MW01181254

WORDS
from the
HEART

Volume I

by

Benjamin E. Thompkins Jr.

DORRANCE
PUBLISHING CO
EST. 1920
PITTSBURGH, PENNSYLVANIA 15235

Dorrance Publishing Co
585 Alpha Drive
Pittsburgh, PA 15238
Visit our website at *www.dorrancebookstore.com*

ISBN: 978-1-6470-2182-5
eISBN: 978-1-6470-2953-1

WORDS
from the
HEART

WE'RE ON A JOURNEY

We're On A Journey, my Friend,

So Enjoy, All of your Days; when they Each, Begin,

Rejoice, in the Fact you were Able; to Suddenly, Wake Up:

For the Reality, of Living; will only Come, Day by Day,

In this, through Time; Knowledge and Understanding, will come your Way,

So in Wisdom, always Try, to take your Steps—

We're On A Journey, can't you See?

And this Trip, Begins; with the Thoughts, We will Perceive,

Our Trip, will be Filled with the Feelings; our Emotions, will Shout:

Can't you See, this Reality, in Thee?

That Each Day, is Lived; by the Thoughts, you Release?

And that your Days, only Appear, One by One—

So Get Up, and take a Stand,

Live, this Life; that's Dwelling, in your Hands,

Live, to be Thankful, for what you Own:

For We're On A Journey, Each Day,

And how we Dwell, from Within, will Honestly Display,

The Future Direction, Our Feet, will have to Walk—

SALT OF THE EARTH

How can I?

Be the Salt Of The Earth?

How, can I Add Flavor, to this World:

It Starts, with the Attitude, I Personally Hold,

The Truth, I See; when it Must, be Told,

It Starts, by Reaching out to my Family, and my Friends—

The Love, I Actually; Live, and Show,

The Compassion, towards Others; I Allow, to Flow,

These Things, must Surely come, from Deep Within:

Then, as I Release Them; while Walking, Here and There,

The Salt, Of The Earth; is being Sprinkled, Throughout the Air,

It's being Tasted, by All of Those, I come to Meet—

Through the Kindness, I Express; when Wrongs, Appear,

Through the Gentleness, I Express; when being Misused, is what I Feel,

These Reactions, are Part of Being, the Salt of the Earth:

And as, I Spend; my Time, in Prayer,

God, will Make me; Truly, Aware,

Where my Salt, is Needed, the Most—

TO THE TWO OF YOU

To The Two Of You, I must Say,

Let your Love, for Each Other; Never, go Astray,

Let your Life, Forever Be, Together as One:

Don't Either, of You; let a Day, go By,

Without You Both, having a Love; that Will, Survive,

Without You Both, Revealing a Passion; that You Each, can Taste—

Don't, you Know; You are to Love, Your Mate?

Which Isn't, Always about your Feelings; but By the Actions, you Create,

It's Based, on Placing Your Mate, before your own Self:

So be Gentle, and Kind; in How, you Relate,

While Understanding, a Truth; that it must be Done, Day to Day,

And Always Forgive, for this will Allow Your Love, to Always Shine—

To The Two Of You, Take It; One Breath, at a Time,

From your Heart, let Your Thoughts be Appreciative; In, your Daily Stride,

Control Your Emotions, when Your Anger, wants to Speak:

For You are Walking, as One; a Gift, from God,

So Face, Your Daily Battles; so Your Relationship, will not Fall,

Know that You Both, are to be for Each Other, a Source for Peace—

A NAME (1)

A Name, I Know; has Come, to Be,

The Ruler, Forever; over All, Human Beings:

This Name, did Die; for You, and Me,

A Name, that will Last; so All of Creation, can be Free—

A Name, so True, it has Endured,

To Seek, out the Life; that One Day, He will Rule:

This Name, is Searching; for You, and for Me,

Waiting, to take Us; to the Place, where He will Be—

A Name, which Turns; All Fears, Away,

Brings Joy, to You; if in His Name, you Personally Claim:

A Faith, He Gives; so your Heart, can be Sure,

When Adversity, Comes; to Hold You, in its Rule—

A Name, that Came; and will Come, Again,

To Take, All of Those; who Believed, in Him:

I Heard, of a Name; called Jesus, The Christ,

I Read, of His Name; in the Instruction Book, for Life—

GOD'S TIMING

God's Timing, does Exist; for You, to Perceive,

It's a Gift, from Above; that Helps You, in your Belief,

For His Timing, must be Wanted, within your Heart:

So Don't, be Impatient; for your Request, to Come,

Stay Focused, on your Daily Journey; Comprehend All, that comes Along,

Allow God's Timing, to be a Perfect Experience, with Each of your Thoughts—

So Always Step, at God's, Personal Pace,

While Learning, to Live; in your Own, Individual Race,

Learn to Walk, on the Path, that you must Walk:

Then Make, All of your Desires; unto Him, Truly Known,

While Growing, in those Things; you Now can Achieve, and Actually Perform,

Allow God, to Overcome the Obstacles, that you will Face—

Be Patient, my Friend; with a True Spirit, in You,

Be Forgiving, and Kind; because this Effects, what God will Do,

Be Diligent, as you Personally; Walk, your Walk:

Then, God's Timing; will be Absolutely Perfect, in your View,

When you Experience Him, in your Soul; making your Thoughts, Brand New,

When you allow His Word, to be the Foundation, within your Heart—

LIKE A CHILD (1)

Like A Child, Lord, I must Be,

Please, Help me; in You, to See,

The Wonder, and the Beauty, of this Earth:

Teach me, how to be Amazed,

At All, of the Beauty; that You, have Made,

Like A Child, let me see You, in my Walk—

Let me Run, Around, and Play,

In My Spirit, Like A Child; let me Truly, Behave,

Let me Reach Out, Only, towards You:

For my Trust, must be Established; in All, You'll Do,

Knowing, You'll Do; Whatever, You must Prove,

Like A Child, I must Depend on You, from my Heart—

In my Mind, You must Stay,

You must Never, Go Astray,

Like A Child, I must Believe in You, without any Doubt:

For Like A Child, I must Come,

Knowing, that You will Never; Leave Me, Alone,

Knowing, You'll Fight My Battles, when they Come About—

JOY AND PAIN

Have you Ever, Experienced, Joy and Pain?

Do you Understand, how They can Lead you; in All, of your Ways?

Do you Realize, how They Both Develop, within your Heart:

For there Cannot, be One; without, the Other,

They Both, will Give you a Direction; in which, to Follow,

From Within, They Both can Teach You, how to Hope—

For Pain, brings out Things; you Wish, weren't There,

Pain, means you're Facing Something; that Makes You, Aware,

That a Certain Reality, has Actually Come; and it's Saddened, your Thoughts:

Yet Joy, when it Comes, will Enlighten You,

To the Truths, that you Learned; when your Pain, was True,

Joy, will Help You Appreciate the Things, you already Own—

So Understand, the Two; there's a Reason, why They Come,

They are Experiences, that will Be; for Each, and Everyone,

And how They're Handled, will Determine the Path; that a Person, will Walk:

For Pain, brings Us Grief; Allowing our Faith, to come Alive,

While Joy, will bring Us Relief; when we've Overcome, a Particular Trial,

And how We Grow, will Actually Depend; on how We Handle, Them Each—

THREE THAT ARE ONE

Happy is the One,

Who knows, the FATHER, and the SON,

Who has THEIR SPIRIT, showing them Personally, how to Exist:

The Three That Are One,

Living, within You; to Keep You, Spiritually Strong,

The Three, who're Reaching Out; to give You, Their Peace—

When Tribulations Appear,

When your Heart, is Seeking; for that Path, to Simple Cheer,

When Confusion, tries to Hold You, with a Strong Grip:

The Three That Are One,

Will Overcome, what you See; no Matter What, you come Upon,

For They Already, have Taken Care, of your Every Need—

Their Power is True,

They will Never, Abandon You,

They will be There, always Establishing You, in Their Ways:

The FATHER, and the SON,

Will Be, the Hope; that Carries, you On,

While the SPIRIT, will Give you THEIR Faith, as a Personal Gift—

YOURSELF

How do you Dwell, from Within?

What Foundation, does your Spirit; Stand on, my Friend?

What Hopes, do you Carry, within your Heart:

For you must Examine, Yourself; in Each, of your Days,

By doing This, you keep Focus; in Establishing, your Ways,

By doing This, you are Able, to Grow Whole—

Do you Understand, the Thoughts, of your Mind?

For the Thoughts, you Release; will Bring those Issues, to Life,

Through your Thoughts, your Feelings and Emotions, will take Shape:

So, you must Examine, Yourself; with Each, of your Steps,

For in Knowing, what you are Doing; you'll have a Direction, to Step,

You can Overcome, your Daily Battles, when they Rise—

So, do you Know Yourself; I must Ask, Again?

Your First Step, is Understanding your Mind; through the Thoughts, you Create,

For you must Realize, the Inner Course, in how you Walk:

Because your Feelings, are for Real,

Responding Only, to the Foundation; you Spiritually, have Built,

So you must Always, keep Renewing, your Personal Thoughts—

I ALWAYS

I Always, had a Prayer,

That Someone, like You; would Wish, to Share,

My Presence, in their Personal, Daily Life:

To Attempt, Together; in making Our Dreams, come True,

To Encourage, Each Other; when Our Hearts, are feeling Blue,

To Tell Each Other, we will Always Be, as we Go About—

I Always, had a Dream, Inside,

That a Person, like You; would Be, by my Side,

That this Person, would Truly Make; my Reality, so Sweet:

For Our Oneness, Together; must Never, let Go,

We must Accept, each Other as We Are; allowing Our Relationship, to Grow,

While Our Hearts, must Trust in Each Other; to Have, sure Peace - -

I Always, Wanted; to be Able, to Say,

Thank You, my Dear; for Coming, my Way,

Thank You, for letting me Step; beside, your Feet:

So I Say, these Words, to let you Know,

That I Love You, my Dear; you're the Only Person, I Adore,

And I'm Thankful, that you Desire Me; as your Own, True Mate—

HE WAS BORN TO BE

He Was Born To Be, a Servant,

To Serve us, in what we Need:

He Was Born To Be, a Warrior,

He would Fight, so we Spiritually, could be Free:

He Was Born To Be, an Innocent Lamb,

To the Slaughter, He would Go:

He Was Born To Be, the King of Kings,

To Rule, when One Day, He would Walk this Earth—

He Was Born To Be, the Sin, we could Release,

His Blood, would Make, All things Whole:

He Was Born To Be, the Giver, of Good Things,

So our Dreams, we One Day, could Hold:

He Was Born To Be, a Power made Available, for Us to Receive,

Allowing Each Person, from Within, to Truly Grow:

He Was Born To Be, the One who would Hang, upon a Tree,

So Death's Power, would Be, no More—

He Was Born To Be, so His Spirit, could be Released,

Giving Life, for Evermore:

He Was Born To Be, A Babe, for You and Me,

So our Lives, could Know, True Joy:

He Was Born To Be, a Path, for our Feet,

To Lead our Steps, when we Personally, would need Hope:

He Was Born To Be, All! we would Ever Need,

Along with His Father, and the One Called, the Holy Ghost—

THE ARMOR OF GOD

The Armor Of God,

When Truly Worn,

Will Scatter, your Enemies, About:

This Armor, so True,

Is there, to Protect; Me, and You,

When Placed On, in Honesty, from the Heart—

Take the HELMET, that must be Worn,

It's a Reminder, of God's Salvation; that your Mind, must Put On,

It's the Reality, of Eternal Life with Him; that your Soul, must Receive:

Also, Understand the BREASTPLATE, you are to Own,

It's God's, Righteous Ways; not the Works, you want to Perform,

It's having His Favor, because your Trust; is in All, He's Achieved—

Then, there Is; the BELT, called TRUTH,

Which Is, the Final Say; in All He wants to Reveal, to Me and You,

It's the Foundation, of His Final Judgement; towards this Reality, called Life:

And when, you Put On; the SHOES, He Prepares,

You'll be Able, to Go Out; and make Others, Aware,

That His Forgiveness, can be for Anyone; if it's Him, they Believe—

There's also, the SHIELD OF FAITH; which is a Gift, that must be Used,

To Block, the Devil's Arrows; to Overcome, his Personal Abuse,

To Stand Firm, so you can Grow, as you Must:

Then, take the SWORD; that You, must Swing,

It must be Swung, in Every Situation; by Claiming the Promises, that you Perceive,

It must be Swung, by Claiming the WORD, that is in your Heart—

The Armor Of God, is something Spiritually, you must Wear,

It's being Polished, when for Others; you Daily, say your Prayers

It's Truly Shines, through the Strength, of your Inner Walk:

For the Devil, my Friend; is to make Sure, you don't Declare,

The LOVE, of God; and how through His SON, He Truly CARES,

So you must Always, wear The Armor, as you Go About —

CHANGE

There's a Change,

That Surely, must Come,

It must Happen, with the Truth Inside, a Person's Heart:

For what, in this Life, do you See?

While you Live, and Daily Stride; in your Own, Spiritual Belief?

What, kind of Life from Within, do you Personally Hold—

Are you in a Relationship, my Friend?

Then ask God, to Draw you Both Closer; by Each, of Your Days End,

Ask Him to Guide you, in this Relationship; as You Both, go About:

Do you See Poverty, in the Streets?

And if you Do, what are you Doing; to Help those People, surely Eat,

What Kind of Change, will you Make; in Helping Others, become Whole—

Those Thoughts, Flowing, within your Mind,

Are you Willing, to Change Them; allowing Yourself, to Spiritually Thrive?

Are you Willing, to Do what you Must; to Establish, some Hope:

For Life, is a Gift; that is being Experienced, through Each Day,

So as Individuals, we must be Willing; to Change, our Personal Ways,

We must Allow God's Love, to be the Reality, that Changes our Hearts—

ENJOY

Enjoy, Each Day,

That will Come, your Way,

Enjoy it, before that Day, is Actually Gone:

For Today, is All; you will Ever, Own,

So Appreciate, the Moments; this Day, will Form,

Soak in the Truths, This Day, will actually Bring—

Enjoy, the Time, you Have,

Don't Allow, your Tribulations; to take You, Off your Path,

Don't Allow Them, to take you Off, your Personal Course:

Just Enjoy, the Flowers; you Daily, do See,

Relax, as the Breeze; Comes, upon Thee,

Realize these Realities, when Each of your Days, are actually Walked—

So Remember, that Today; is All, you can Perceive,

For Yesterday, is Gone; Never Again, to be Seen,

And as for Tomorrow, it may Never, come Along:

So Enjoy, the Time; you Daily, can Breathe,

For God, has Given you Life; that is being Experienced, for Free,

So Enjoy, Each of your Moments, One by One—

UNDERSTAND THE BATTLE

Understand The Battle, you are In,

Don't let those Moments, of Deep Despair; Hinder you, my Friend,

Don't let your Pain, be the Foundation, on which you Walk:

Just Realize, this War; has Already, been Won,

For in Each, of your Battles; there's Victory, to be Owned,

If you Understand, how the Lord, has Set you Free—

So much, on this Earth, is there to Enjoy,

Yet what, would be your Reason; when Despair, takes your Hope?

What, would be your Reason; for These Feelings, to Flow with Ease:

Though, there is a Time to Mourn; for certain Events, that will Be,

Yet certain, Situations; should Never bring Sadness, to Thee,

So Understand, the Personal Flow, of your Thoughts—

For Someone, Fought a Fight; to Give you, True Hope,

To take, All you would Feel; so your Emotions, could have Joy,

To Forgive, All of your Wrongs; so you would not Live, in Guilt:

So Understand, The Battle; you are Experiencing, from Within,

Grow, in God's Words; so you can Realize, what's been Fulfilled,

Then Receive, each of the Promises; that He, has Wrote—

WHAT DOES GOD DO

What Does God Do?

For Those, whose Heart; is Strong, and True?

For Those, who have Accepted Him, upon this Earth:

He Measures, out Their Faith; Allowing Them, to Believe,

He Seals Them, with His Spirit; so His Self, can be Seen,

He Gives Them His Word, so Spiritually, they can have Hope—

He brings Peace, their Way,

Through, the Understanding; they Live In, Each Day,

Through, the Truths they Hold onto; while they're Renewing, their Thoughts:

He'll make Them, the Head; and Not, the Tail,

He'll Answer, All their Prayers; if His Will, is what they Claim,

He'll Give them Wisdom, that will Keep their Souls, from being Lost—

What Does God Do?

For Those, who Know; the Cross, is True?

For Those, who Bare Witness of His Son; and the Reason, for His Death:

He'll allow, certain Trials; to Come, their Way,

So the Strength, they'll Need; can be Established, and not Stray,

He'll allow Tribulations, so their Patience, can be Formed—

Joy, will Be; a Part, of their Lives,

Eternity with Him, will be Knowledge; that Helps them, to Thrive,

GOD'S LOVE, will be the Foundation, on which they Walk:

What Does God Do?

Day by Day, He'll See, them Through,

Day by Day, He'll Watch Over Them, as they go About—

THE LOVE WE MUST SHARE

The Love We Must Share

Must Be, from Our Hearts; Each Day, that is There,

Our Love, must be the Foundation, in how We Walk:

To Place, the Other; before, their Own Self,

To be an Ear, when Their Voice; Needs, to Confess,

Those Concerns, That Swirl Deep, from Their Thoughts—

The Love We Must Share,

Must Surely, be Something; We Daily, do Wear,

Our Love, must Overcome the Adversity; that can Steal, our Hopes:

For We must Appreciate, the Reality; of our One, True Mate,

This Reality, must be a Treat; that We Daily, can Taste,

Each Day, We must Grow in Their Love, as it's being Expressed—

The Love We Must Share,

This Love, must always Show; that We Truly, do Care,

This Love, must be a Truth that's Released, from Our Hearts:

For this, will Come; through the Words, that We Speak,

The Way, We Act; when We Sometimes, don't Agree,

Our Love, will be Established through the Actions, We Personally Create—

WE'RE HUMAN

We're Human, am I Right?

It shouldn't Matter, if we're Black, or White,

It shouldn't Matter, where we were Born, upon this Earth:

Are we Not, Supposed to Walk; Side, by Side?

Allowing, the Human Race, to Actually Thrive?

Are we Not, Supposed to Encourage Each Person, to Stand in Hope—

When the Sun, does Shine?

Doesn't, its Brightness Touch; Whomever, is Alive?

Doesn't, each Person Feel its Power, and its Warmth:

How about the Birds, when they Sing?

Aren't, their Songs Meant; for each Person, who would Breathe?

Isn't their Music, meant for each Person; who would be Upon, the Earth—

We're Human, are we Not?

Isn't, this World Meant; for each Person, who comes About?

Is not, the Blue Sky a Treat; for All, who Exist:

Am I Not, my Brother's Keeper?

Should not, the Strong; Uphold Those, that are Weaker?

Shouldn't each Person, take the Steps in Caring, for their Fellowman—

THE VICTORY IS YOURS

The Victory Is Yours, I Say,

So get Up, each Morning; and let your Heart, Proclaim,

The Appreciation, of Knowing you are Alive, upon this Earth:

Oh, if Each Person, could See,

That in each Day, a Way to Deal with their Trials; is There, to be Seen,

A Way to Overcome, is There, to be Known—

The Victory Is Yours, to Perceive,

It's There, to Grab a Hold Of; it's There, to Receive,

It's There, through the Knowledge and Understanding; you Actually, do Walk:

For Adversity, is True, my Friend,

But there's Power, to Own; as you Stride, to be Free,

There's Hope, that You can Live; when Your Troubles, come About—

The Victory Is Yours, to Stay,

So when Problems, Appear; give them to the Lord, so He can Display,

The Might, He wants to Give; to Strengthen, your Heart:

For God, can Use You; Right where, you Spiritually Are,

He'll Lift you Up, unto Himself; giving you the Ability, to Walk your Call,

He'll give you His Spirit, so you can Proclaim; how He Gave you, His Rest—

KNOW YOURSELF FROM WITHIN

Know Yourself From Within,

Are you Led Around, in a Bad Way; by Someone, who calls you Friend?

Are you Living, just to Please, Everyone Else:

Don't Try, and Keep Up; with All, the Others,

For in, the End; you must Be, your Own Person,

You must Be, a Person who is Content, with their Own Self—

Stand, on your Own, Two Feet,

Don't Depend, on Someone or a Thing; to Be, your Final Peace,

Just Enjoy, each Personal Moment, as you go About:

For in, your Present Moment; you May Not Be, where you Want,

So Stay Focused, on the Path; that you Now, can only Walk,

Allow Time, to Establish the Foundation, in where you Want to Be—

Know Yourself, From Within, Each Day,

Control, your Thoughts; as they Flow, your Way,

Realize your Thoughts, Create the Realities; you Personally, will Seek:

So, what Attitude do you Show, when you Arise?

Are you an Example, of How; a Person, should Survive?

Or, are you Hindering your Self; by the Way, you actually Live—

A BOOK THAT WAS WRITTEN

A Book That Was Written, was to Let, Everyone Know,

The Story, of Life; and How, it would Unfold,

It Tells the Ways, in how God would Reach Out, to All who would Breathe:

You will Learn, of Great Things; such As, His Personal Love,

It Tells you, of His Dreams; and How, He can Fulfill Yours,

This Book was Written, for Every, Human Being—

Instructions, are Given; in How, to Stay True,

Also Angels, are Talked about; and the Works, they do for You,

Real History, is even Talked about; that took Place, on the Earth:

Words of Peace, and Joy; are There, to Know,

An Eternal, Future; is Even, Foretold,

The Reality of Life, will be made Clear, before your Own Self—

A Book, That Was Written; was Created, by the Living God,

He would Use, Certain People; to Speak, His Words out Loud,

He would Use a Human, to Write, All He Felt:

For the Things, that were Written; didn't Come, from HUMAN THOUGHT,

They Came, from HIS SPIRIT; who actually Lived, in Their Hearts,

God's Spirit, would tell Them to Write, what He wanted Expressed—

The Words, which God Spoke; are So, Very True,

They're In A Book, That Was Written; Meant Only, for You,

It's a Book, that Truly, must be Read:

For it's Called, the Bible; to You, and I,

If Anything, the Prophesies Spoken; must Surely, Be Realized,

For ALL that is Written, is about to Finally, be FULFILLED—

GRAFTED

Grafted, in the Vine, I am,

I've become, the Seed, of Abraham,

I've been Saved, by the Blood, of the Lamb:

For He's Made Me, a Part; of the Kingdom, He Owns,

Before God, I now can Stand; coming Boldly, before His Throne,

I Now, can make Known to Him, my Personal Request—

He's My Advocate, before God; Testifying, of my Faith,

Because of This, I have Become; an Ambassador, of His Grace,

I Represent Him, in this Present, Earthly Realm:

For He Stood, in Our Place; becoming SIN, for ALL of MAN,

Now We, can Receive God's Goodness; Allowing His Ways, to be Our Plan,

Now He, can be the Path, on which We Walk—

To Those who Believe,

Then Know, that His Spirit; Dwells, within Thee,

Know, that the Lamb's Sacrifice, has made you Whole:

So Walk Strong, in Your Heart; Understanding in Him, just who You Are,

Realize, who Represents You; before, Almighty God,

Then Know, that you have been Grafted, into Place—

LIVE

Live, for the Reality, of Today,

Don't let, these Moments, Slip Away,

Let each Moment, you can Taste, have some Hope:

For Each Day, you Hold,

Will Develop, the Foundation; your Future, will Show,

It Develops the Path, you Daily, will actually Walk—

And how, can Each Moment, be Seen?

Through, the Thoughts; that are Leading, your Feet,

For through your Thoughts, Each of your Personal Moments, will be Felt:

So Live, in the Reality; that Currently, is Known,

For it's, the Only Time; your Hopes, can be Owned,

It's the Only Time, you can Reach Out to Achieve, that Certain Dream—

So Smell, the Flowers; that Exist, before You,

Enjoy, the Sunset; each One, you can View,

Taste the Breeze, when it's Blowing, Everywhere:

For Today, is All; you will Actually, ever Know,

So Live, in the Moment; like it's the Last One, you will Hold,

Live in the Present, like it's the Last Day, you will ever See—

ALL I KNOW

I really, don't Know,

What Tomorrow, will Bring,

Only the Moment, that Currently, is being Shown:

For Right Now, is the only Time; I am Able, to Breathe,

And what I do Today, will Show Me; what I must Do, to Achieve,

Today, will Determine how Far; I Still, must Walk—

All I know,

Is the Time, that Already Exists,

The Present Moment, I Actually, do Own:

For it's in the Present, that I must Grow,

This, will Allow; my Foundation, to be Whole,

This, will Allow Me, to Know Spiritual Peace—

Each New Dawn, will Bring,

A Reality, wanting Joy; even though Misery, may be Seen,

Each Day, will bring a New Truth; that We Each, must Hold:

So where, is your Heart; and Mind, my Friend?

All I Know, is that Life; is a Gift, to ALL HUMANS,

And that You should Treat, Each and Every Person; as You, would Want—

THIS LOVE WE HOLD

This Love We Hold,

Shouldn't it, be more Precious; than the Reality, of Pure Gold?

Shouldn't it, be Worth more than All the Silver, that is on the Earth:

For Our Relationship, must always be True,

Overcoming All, this World; will Put, Us Through,

Overcoming the Damages, that even We, will Personally Create—

This Love We Hold,

Must have, a Foundation; on which, to Grow,

It must have a Path, on which our Oneness, can Actually Relate:

For We Both, must put Each Other; before, Our Own Self,

While Being There, when it's Required; becoming Strength, for Our Mate,

Always Being There, so our Personal Love, can Always Form—

So let Each Day, for Us Be; Truly, Brand New,

In Our Life, Together; in All, We will Do,

Let Each Day, Truly Accomplish; what We're Suppose, to Taste:

For at Times, We may Stumble; and Spiritually, may Fall,

But as One, Side by Side; in Every Situation, We can Thrive,

If We have Accepted, Each Other, as Our Only Mate—

MY HANDS ARE MADE FOR

My Hands Are Made For Grabbing,

To Pull the Ones, I Love, to me Near:

My Hands Are Made For Working,

So I can Provide, for the Family, I hold Dear:

My Hands Are Made For Searching,

Obtaining Knowledge, so I can Grow, in Spiritual Might:

My Hands Are Made For Playing,

So I can Enjoy, those Special Moments, in my Life—

My Hands Are Made for Wiping,

To Dry the Eyes, of Someone, that's in Tears:

My Hands Are Made For Clapping,

So I can Participate, with Those, that are in Cheer:

My Hands Are Made For Touching,

Allowing me to Appreciate, what I Hold, that's in my Sight:

My Hands Are Made For Praying,

To Honor the Lord, who is the Foundation, in My Life—

IN THE MIST

During your Moments, of Deep Despair,

With no Power, or Might; to Place On, and Wear,

When it Seems Like, you have no Strength; to Step, your Steps:

In the Mist, of This; God, does Stand,

By your Side, through His Spirit; He will Take You, by the Hand,

He will Lead You, so you can Experience; His Power, and Rest—

Yes, Trials and Tribulations; will Come, your Way,

This, is a Reality; that Each Person, will have to Face,

This Truth, must be Realized, Deep in your Heart:

Yet, In The Mist of All of This; God, is already There,

He is Fighting, the Fight; Each Person, will Bare,

If their Hope, Depends on the Power, that He Gives Out—

So don't, Give Up; when your Back, is against the Wall,

Hold, your Head High; Knowing God, will Handle it All,

Know, He's in Control, of your Personal Fate:

And while, you are Walking; in the Mist, of a Storm,

Understand, when You're at your Weakest; God the Father, is Truly Strong,

Know, that He'll Always Strengthen you; in what Ever, you Face—

THE MOMENTS IN THIS DAY

The Moments In This Day,

Taste, their Presence; while they Flow, your Way,

Realize, this Special Reality, within your Heart:

It Shouldn't Matter, what you Personally, are going Through,

For each Moment, you Hold; will Reveal, its own Truth,

So Learn to See, Each of your Moments, as they Come—

For This, must Start; in your Mind, my Friend,

So How, do your Thoughts Flow; from Deep, Within?

What Attitude, is being Formed; that you Evidentially, will Shout:

Just, Understand; the Power, of your Mind,

For each Person, this must Be; a Part, of their Daily Life,

For how a Person Thinks, will Reveal the Attitude, in how they'll Walk—

The Moments In This Day,

Are the Only Experiences, Relating to Living; you Actually, will Taste,

And in each of these Moments, certain Thoughts, will be Bouncing About:

So let the Knowledge, and Understanding of God; always Grow, in your Mind,

Then Stop, and Understand this Knowledge; that's Dwelling, Inside,

Then let Wisdom Lead You, in All you Do; and All, you will Say—

YOUR JOY

What's Your Joy, based On, my Friend?

What Foundation, do you Stand Upon; from Deep, Within?

What Realities, are you Holding onto, inside your Heart:

Are you Waiting, for an Event; or a Person, to Appear?

To Bring, you Joy; which will Allow You, to Live?

Are you Waiting, for Something to Suddenly Happen, in your Earthly Walk—

Life is Awesome, I must Say,

So Each Day, must be Precious; in its Own, Special Way,

For Each Day, has a Particular Joy; that You, can be Shout:

So Don't, let Something; have to be Given, to You,

Truly Enjoy, the Little Things; that you Daily, can Do,

Realize the Little Things, must be the Realities; that Inspires, your Heart—

Your Joy, is it Spiritually, for Real?

Do you Appreciate, your Trials; while you're Climbing, up that Hill?

Do you Appreciate, Each of Your Victories; the Ones you Actually, can Wear:

So don't let, some Future Thing; be Your Joy, in this Life,

Stay Focus, on the Little Things; that now Exist, in your Sight,

Know each Day, can Lead to a Brighter Future, if it's Properly Worn—

HOW I ADORE

How I Adore You, my Dear,

I want You, in my Life; each Day, that Appears,

Each Day, I want You Only, for Myself:

For there Is, no Other; for Me, to Enjoy,

It's towards You, my Dear; I want to Give, so Much More,

It's towards You, I want my Love, to be Expressed—

How I Adore You, I Say,

You are a Joy, I Have; that's a Part, of my Day,

You are the Person, who Brings Out of Me, my Very Best:

How I Adore You, in my View,

You Fill a Space, in my Life; that I Once, Personally Knew,

For You are Always, in my Heart; which Gives, me Rest—

How I Adore, Your Spiritual Grace,

You are a Blessing, to Me; that Stands, before my Face,

You are a Gift, that I Daily, want to Hold:

How I Adore, this Love, You Always Display,

You are a Dream, come True; that God has Bought, my Way,

You are the Answer, that He has Given, from my Personal Request—

THE ANOINTING OF GOD

The Anointing Of God,

Is the Reality, of His Grace,

This Anointing, is there for All People, to actually Own:

It's Meant, to let you Know; that He's, Forgiven You,

To Show, in your Every Need; that He'll Always, See you Through,

To let you Know, you have a Future; by Following, His Steps—

Oh, the Beauty, of it All,

When you See, your Fears; Begin, to Fall,

When you Taste, the Spiritual Victory, of His Inner Rest:

His Anointing, is so Sure,

That the Understanding, of Your Faith; will be Seen, as a Gift,

And that it's Measured Out, so you Personally; can Fulfill, your Call—

To Perceive, before you Receive; Relating to a Wish, coming True,

To Rejoice, In your Trials; while you are Walking, Each One Through,

To do Your All, while He is Helping You; through Each, of your Test:

The Anointing, of God; is So, Very Real,

It's being Poured, Upon You; when you Receive, what He's Revealed,

It's being Poured, because you Depend Upon Him, within Yourself—

LIFE IS ONLY NOW

Life Is Only Now,

Through your Heart, in this Moment; do you Really, See How?

In your Thoughts, is this Reality, before your Face:

For the Moments, of Each Day; are so Precious, my Friend,

So don't Wait, for Something to Happen; to Bring you, a Certain Cheer,

Let this Day, have its own Purpose, in your Personal Walk—

So ask Yourself, about the Goals; you Now, do Hold?

And if None, are you on a Path; that will Help you, to Grow?

Do you have a Foundation, that you Daily, can take your Steps:

Is there an Influence, that Shouldn't, be There?

Or Maybe, a Bad Situation; you must Stand Up to, and Actually Bare?

Are there Obstacles, that you must Face, in your Personal Quest—

For Life Is Only Now, I Say,

So Realize, your Blessings; that are to be Seen, in Each Day,

Appreciate those Individuals, who are Supporting You, in this Earthly Walk:

And take Control, of those Thoughts; that are Dwelling, in your Mind,

Treat Others Good, from your Heart; even, as You would Like,

Let your Kindness, be Something that's Seen, as you go About—

DO NOT WEEP

Do Not Weep, for Me,

For I've Gone, to Be; with the Father, of Peace,

I've Gone, to Stand before Him, and His Begotten Son:

I'm in, the Presence; of the Angels, Right Now,

So you, Straighten Up; and Hold, your Head High,

For I'm Dwelling, with the One who Created, the Human Race—

Do Not Weep, I Say,

For God has Promised, we'll be Together; in Another, Realm of Life,

In Time, we will be Together, Face to Face:

So Go Out, and Do; what you Know, You must Do,

Make Sure, His Spirit; is Truly Dwelling, within You,

So in a Certain Time, We can be Together, in a Holy Place—

Do Not Weep, my Family and Friends,

Because the Lord, has called Me; to Be, with Him,

For the Number, of my Days have Come; and Now, they are Gone:

So Keep, your Hearts, Strong and True,

Then Join Me, One Day; in His Glory, Too,

So Do Not Weep, just Understand; that I've, Gone Home—

WHAT ARE THEY SUPPOSED TO DO?

What Are They Supposed To Do?

When it comes Down, to a Relationship; between, the Two?

When it comes Down, to Revealing Their Love, towards their Mate:

For so Many Things, can go Wrong,

That can Destroy, a Relationship; Right Where, It must Form,

That can Uproot, whatever Truth; They're Suppose, to Face—

So how, can a Man; and Woman, be True?

In Overcoming, the Obstacles; that They, will Go Through?

To have a Foundation, on which They Both, can Daily Step:

They First, must Accept their Mate; for Who, they Are,

Knowing, They'll make Mistakes; and Sometimes, even Fall,

Knowing, that Forgiveness, must Lead the Way—

They must Do, their own Part; so the Relationship, can Grow,

For Neither, can Do; what the Other, must Perform,

They must use Wisdom, so They Each, can Relate:

For Both, will have Issues; that Will, be Shown,

So They must Understand, the Good; that the Other, will Put On,

They must Believe, in the Other Person; who's a Part, of their Fate—

What Are They Supposed To Do?

To make, their Partnership Ripen; like Grapes, in Season Due?

To Enjoy, their Togetherness; which They Both, must Shape:

They must Place, Their Partner; before, Their Own Self,

They must Love, Unconditionally; while they Face, what Life Creates,

They must be Gentle, with the Words; that They Want, to Speak—

I REALIZE

I Realize, that Life,

Consists, of Many Things,

That there is so Much, for Each Person, to Learn:

For it's Full, of Mystery,

It can Be, an Adventure; if a Person Allows, it to Be,

There's so Much, in this Life, to be Known—

I Realize, the Stars; Twinkling, in the Night Sky,

I Realize, that Nature; is Meant, to Daily Thrive,

I Realize, so many People are Starving, in the Streets:

I Realize, that War; is Keeping the Human Race, from having Peace,

Yet, when a Child is Born; I Realize the Joy, that is being Released,

I Realize, the Variety of Emotions; this World, does Shine—

But I Realize, something Else; which Must, be Seen,

It Relates, to Each; and Every, Human Being,

It Relates, to Every Person; who would have Life, upon this Earth:

That being Alive, is a Gift; that God has Given, for Free,

And the Power, of Our Spiritual Life; is how our Minds, will Perceive,

The Realities We must Face, and how We Handle them; while In, this World—

LIFE IS (1)

Life Is a Challenge, that's Full; of Ups, and Downs,

Life Is Joy, that's Flowing, All Around:

Life Is Each Day, with Each Step, that We Take,

Life Is Right Now, at this Moment, in this Very Time—

Life Is a Dream, wanting Something, to Come True,

Life Is the Present, while Wondering what the Future, Holds for You:

Life Is a Shadow, following, Everywhere You Go,

Life Is Today, and Not, Tomorrow—

Life Is Hope, that's Dwelled On, in your Own Way,

Life Is Reality, always Wondering, why it Came:

Life Is a Gift, Given, to You and Me,

Life Is for Free, Each Day, We can Breathe—

Life Is an Instant, each one Coming, when the Others Fade,

Life Is in our Mind, and the Fantasies, we Create:

Life Is from the Heart, always being Expressed, by how We Talk,

Life Is What We are, with Each Tick, of the Clock—

Life Is a Script, being Written Out, Each Day,

Life Is a Play, that Each Person Performs, in their Own Way:

Life is God, and the Love, He Proclaims,

Life Is His Son, the Love, He Made—

STAY FOCUSED

Stay Focused, from Within,

Don't be Tossed, Up and Down, my Friend,

Don't Walk around, in your Heart, feeling Lost:

For Life, has so much to Offer, Me and You,

But what we Receive, will Depend; on How, we View,

The Realities, Our Heart Perceives; that's From, Our Thoughts—

Stay Focused, in your own Way,

Reach Out, and Do; what you Know is Good, in Each Day,

Reach Out to Fulfill, those Certain Dreams; that are In, Your Heart:

For don't, you Know, you can only Do?

Those Things, you Desire; or what you Wish, to come True?

So Stay Focused, on your Path, that Must be Walked—

Just be Strong, in your Mind, my Friend,

For through It, you can See; a Purpose, and an End,

In your Mind, your Personal Attitude, will take Shape:

So, Stay Focused, for your Own Sake,

For this Very Moment, is the Only Time; you Actually, can Display,

Those Personal Desires, that Dwell Deep, within your Heart—

I AM

I Am the Wind, that Blows Everywhere,

I Am a Tree, giving Shade; when the Sun, does Glare,

I Am the Reason, that You Are, a Human Being:

I Am the Life, that is Seen; as You Live, in Each Day,

I Am the One, who can Keep; Your Hopes, from going Astray,

I Am the Strength, that You Daily, will only Need—

I Am the Answer, to Whatever; Human Kind, will Discover,

I Am the One, who Existed; before, there were any Others,

I Am the Way, for You to have Peace, which will Give you Relief:

I Am the Source, of Eternal Joy,

I Am the One, who can Make; Your Fears, no More,

I Am the Love, that Each Person, should Receive—

I Am the MAKER, of ALL; that IS, called LIFE,

I Am the One, who Was; then I Created, All Others,

I Am the Knower, of Each Destiny, that Comes to Be:

I Am the One, called JESUS; the Only, True CHRIST,

I Am the Way, for a Person; to have the Power, to Survive,

I am the One, for Each Person to Know, and then Receive—

SIDE BY SIDE

Side By Side, We must Be,

Facing, Our Trials; while We're Seeking, Inner Peace,

Facing, the Tribulations; this Life, will Form:

For Together, We must Grow,

Experiencing, Life; as Each Day Burns, its own Glow,

Tasting Life, as Each Moment, is being Released—

Side By Side, my Dear,

Our Dreams, must Never; Come, to an End,

In Our Life, We must keep Reaching Out; to Fulfill, Our Hopes:

For In, Our Hearts; We Both, must Know,

That if We are There, for Each Other; Our Love, will Only Grow,

Our Love, will Create the Foundation, on which We Walk—

Side By Side, You and I,

Our Relationship, can Last; if Our Commitment, is not a Lie,

If We can Forgive, then Both of Our Spirits; will Always, be Free:

For Life, will come to Us; One Day, at a Time,

And if We Place, Each Other First; Our Oneness, can Only Thrive,

Our Togetherness, will Know the Reality; of what a Relationship, Means—

COMPREHEND THIS DAY

Comprehend This Day,

Don't, let its Beauty; from Your Eyes, Slip Away,

Don't, let this Reality You See, go Spiritually Lost:

For those Things, in Your Life; which at the Moment, are a Heavy Weight,

Cannot Be, the Main Focus; in how Your Day, will be Displayed,

They cannot Be, a Part of Your Foundation, in how you Stride—

Comprehend This Day, you Presently, do Know,

For in it, your Dreams; can Actually, be Owned,

Your Dreams, will have a Chance, to be Fulfilled:

So Comprehend, This Day; for Yourself, I Say,

While Realizing, a Truth; that Tribulations, will come Your Way,

Realize Your Tribulations, Develop the Faith; which Strengthens, your Heart—

Also, take a Hold; of the Thoughts, that you Perceive,

For the Thoughts, that you Release; will Decide, if your Heart Believes,

From your Heart, your Emotions; will Walk, Their Walk:

So, Just Comprehend This Day; while you Still, can Call it Your Own,

Understand, how you Spiritually Stand; so you'll have a Clear Direction, to Follow,

Appreciate the Reality, of being Alive; that Each Day, will Bring—

WHY WORRY

Why Worry, about Something; you Personally, can't Control?

Don't, let Yourself; go Down, in Your Soul,

Keep Strong, by the Way, you Spiritually Walk:

For Life, will be Full; of Many, Ups and Downs,

So don't, let your Heart; sink Down, to the Ground,

Be Established, right where you Stand, within your Thoughts—

Why Worry, I Say?

Didn't, the Sun Rise; Upon You, Today?

Aren't you Alive, by the Simple Fact; you were Able, to Wake Up:

For Don't, you Know; that This, could be the Day?

To When, your Last Steps; could Come, your Way?

So allow your Mind, to Appreciate this Life; as you Live, and Talk—

Why Worry, my Friend?

Always, Stay Focus; from Deep, Within,

Stay Focus, on the Present Moments, within Your Heart:

And how, do you Keep Yourself; from Straying, in the Present Time?

By Knowing, you may not See; Tomorrow, Shine its Shines,

By Knowing, you may not See the Ones, you actually Love—

AM I MY BROTHER'S KEEPER?

Am I My Brother's Keeper?

When their Heart, is Down and Blue:

Am I My Brother's Keeper?

When they Need, a Different View:

Am I My Brother's Keeper?

When they're Seeking, for a Listening Ear:

Am I My Brother's Keeper?

When I Know, they Need, me Near—

Am I My Brother's Keeper?

By Helping them, Face their Life:

Am I My Brother's Keeper?

By Always, being Nice:

Am I My Brother's Keeper?

In All, I Say and Do:

Am I My Brother's Keeper?

Oh Yes! This is what God Wants, from You and I—

TOWARDS YOUR MATE

Towards Your Mate,

Show your Love, for Them; in your Own, Special Way,

Let Them Know, They're the Only Person; that's Filling, Your Thoughts:

Don't, let a Day, go By,

Without, you Holding Them Near; while Helping Them, to Realize,

That Their Presence, is Truly Appreciated, in Your Life—

Towards Your Mate, I must Say,

Let your Love, be Unconditional; so the Relationship, will not Stray,

Shall Their Life, See your Goodness, within Their Heart:

For don't you Know, you must Be; Their Strong, Right Hand?

Enabling Them, Daily; to Spiritually, Try and Stand,

Allowing Them, to Rest on your Shoulder; while They Relieve, their Thoughts—

Always, show Mercy; from your Spirit, be Kind,

Watch, the Words you Speak; for the Wrong Ones, can Damage Their Minds,

Always Forgive, because You Both, will Make Mistakes:

So, Towards Your Mate; What, are You to Do?

Just take it, Day by Day; for it's the Only Time, you can View,

The Reality, of Their Love for You; that's In, Their Heart—

THE TIME WE HAVE

The Time We Have,

Must be Precious, in Our Hands,

For each Moment, must have a Meaning, Within our Hearts:

As Our Days, go By,

In Each, of Our Minds; We Both, must Realize,

Our Personal Love, towards each Other, as We Go About—

To be, the Other's Foundation; when One of Us, is in Need,

Then Our Time, must Create the Building Blocks; that Together, We can See,

That Spiritual Growth, We will Experience; when We Walk, Our Walk:

For You, are the Desire; making Up, my Personal Thoughts,

Without You, being with Me; a Part of Me, will be Lost,

Without You, my Personal Life, will not be Whole—

So, with The Time We Have, my Dear,

We must Live It, very Wisely; so Our Love, can be Real,

We must Live It, so Our Relationship, can Always Grow:

Because it's You, and I; Forever, my Friend,

Let's not Take, for Granted; the Love We Share, from Within,

Let Us have a Bond, that will Allow Us to Be, Forever in Love—

I HAVE NO SAY

I Have No Say,

In what Life, will Bring, my Way,

I have No Say Lord, in What, will Come:

For my Life, belongs to You,

You Took it, Away; the Moment, I was Approved,

You Took It, when I Accepted, Your Begotten Son—

So, when my Trials, Appear,

You will use Them, to Draw Us Closer; so You, can be Near,

You will use Them, so We can become Stronger; as We Stand, as One:

For there's a Joy, You have for Me, each Day,

Like the Fact, of me Knowing; You will Always, Remain,

Yet, I Have No Say; in what You Do, to Fulfill my Hopes—

For I Gave, my Life Over, to You,

So Your Promises, for Me; could All, come True,

So Your Grace, could Bring to Me, my Spiritual Rest:

For I Have No Say, in what You will do Lord,

I have No Choice, the Choice, is Up to You,

I Have No Say, in how You will Show Me, Your Personal Love—

DO WHAT YOU CAN DO

Do What You Can Do,

Take the Time, in Each Day; to Surely, View,

This Life, you Personally Own, upon the Earth:

For the Dreams, you Hold Inside,

Can be Real, if you Only; would Stop, and Realize,

That you are to See Them, as If They Already, were Actually Yours—

Be Patient, towards those Things; that you Hope, to Achieve,

Have Goals, within your Heart; then Reach Out, so They can Be,

Step on the Path, that You, can Only Walk:

Then, Do What You Can Do,

Work, to Accomplish; what You Set Out, to Prove,

Have that Hope, which will Enable You, to Always Step—

Have a Truth, that You Always, must Keep Alive,

Always, allow your Dreams; to Flow Continually, in your Mind,

Never let These Things, from Within, come to a Halt:

And while, you are Reaching; for These Realities, to come True,

Know, that in Each Day; God will Personally, see You Through,

So Do, What You Can Do; so He can Direct, Your Walk—

HOW DO YOU TALK

How Do You Talk, to Those, that are Near?

Do you Speak, your Words; so the Other Person, can Hear?

Do you Say Words, that enable a Person, to Stand in Hope:

Oh, the Words; that We Each, do Sing,

Do Those, who Listen; Hear, the Right Tune?

When your Words, to Them, are being Spoke—

Are you Saying, Words; that are Gentle, and Kind?

Or, are you Sharp and Harsh; when your Words, do Shine?

What Kind of an Attitude, before Others, is being Shown:

For what, you Truly Are; will One Day, be Known

So Speak, Words of Wisdom; so Peace, can be Sown,

For what you Sow, you will One Day, have to Reap—

So, How Do You Talk?

Do you Speak, so that Others; can Grow, in Their Thoughts?

Do you Speak, so that Maybe; they can Sense, some Peace:

For an Awesome Gift, has been Given; to You, and to Me,

It's the Reality, of Our Spirit; and the Words, that We Speak,

So How Do You Talk, in Each of Your Days, from Your Heart—

FOR IT TO BE

In Order, For It To Be,

To where Our Love, can Flow, Continually,

To where Our Hearts, can Walk Together, in Spiritual Might:

We Both, must be Willing; to Do, Our Own Part,

Which is to Place, the Other; before, Our Own Heart,

Allowing a Foundation, for Our Relationship, to Actually Thrive—

To Always, Be; from Within, Renewed,

There's a Truth, We Both; Surely, must View,

That there can Be, no Other Person Dwelling, Deep in Our Hearts:

For Our Oneness, to Stand Strong,

We must Know, by how We Listen; about Our Mate's, Needs and Wants,

We must Seek, to Obtain the Things, they Desire to Receive—

For It To Be, Always, WE,

For It To Be, US TOGETHER; just You, and Me,

Then Know there's a Truth, that We must Hold, in our Personal Walk:

That Life, will come to Us, Day by Day,

With Each Day, being the Moment; We Only, can Display,

The True Love, We have for Each Other, within Our Hearts—

GOD WILL PROVIDE

God Will Provide,

Just, like He Does; for the Birds, in the Sky,

Just, like He Sends the Rains; to Feed, the Earth:

For In, what Ever; You, may Need,

He'll make Sure, it's There; for You, to Receive,

He'll make Sure, that you'll Get, All you Must—

God Will Provide,

True, Spiritual Strength; so You, can Survive,

He'll give Wisdom, so you can Decide, your next Step:

Through your Times, of Trouble; and Great, Despair,

When it Seems, like you can No Longer; Stand Up, and Bear,

He will Deliver you, with His Power, to Ease Your Thoughts—

God Will Provide,

All, the Tools you'll Need; to See, His True Light,

Even Your Faith, which will enable your Hope, to Actually Spread:

He also, will send His Spirit; to Constantly, Renew your Mind,

His Spirit, will Lead you to His Word; so His Truth, can Enlighten your Eyes,

So the Cross, can have that Special Meaning, with your Every Step—

PATIENCE AND FAITH

Patience and Faith,

Must always Be,

Side by Side, Established, within Our Hearts:

For those Hopes, in Which, We Hold,

Will not, be Able; to Truly, Grow,

If These Two, are not being Developed, within Our Thoughts—

Patience, and Faith; must Go, Hand and Hand,

For They Fight, those Situations; trying to Destroy, the Hopes we Plan,

They are Tools, that Enable Us to Survive, upon this Earth:

For PATIENCE, through Time; will Make Our Purpose, Clear and True,

While FAITH, is Knowing Our Request Will Be; before it Exist, in Our View,

And it's Together, They must be Established, within Our Hearts—

Patience and Faith, must be Lived, Day by Day,

Because we Never, really Know; what God will Allow, to Come our Way,

We Never Know, what will Try to Hinder, our Daily Walk:

So Realize, in your Heart; the Personal Direction, you must Take,

While Knowing, in your Mind; the Inner Images, you Create,

Allow Patience, to be a Part of your Faith; so His Son, can Help you Thrive—